THE MYSTERIOUS
MYSTERIES OF THE
ROSARY

Scriptural Meditations for
Pope John Paul II's
Mysteries of Light

Paulist Press
New York/Mahwah, N.J.

Scripture extracts are taken from the New Revised Standard Version, copyright © 1989, by the Division of Christian Education of the National Council of the Churches of Christ in the United States of America and reprinted by permission of the publisher.

Extracts from Pope John Paul II's Apostolic Letter *Rosarium Virginis Mariae* are taken from the electronic file of that document at http://www.vatican.va.

Cover design by Diego Linares
Book design by Lynn Else
Interior illustrations by Frank Sabatté, C.S.P.

Library of Congress Cataloging-in-Publication Data

 The new luminous mysteries of the Rosary : scriptural meditations for Pope John Paul II's Mysteries of Light.
     p. cm.
  ISBN: 0-8091-5219-3 (alk. paper)
  1. Rosary.
  BX2163 .N49 2003
  242'.74—dc21

                                              2003007777

Published by Paulist Press
997 Macarthur Boulevard
Mahwah, New Jersey 07430

www.paulistpress.com

Printed and bound in the United States of America

THE MYSTERIES OF LIGHT

The Rosary, with its mysteries of the life of Jesus as our Savior and Redeemer, has been one of the most highly treasured of all Catholic practices since the end of the twelfth century. Not only does it provide a continuous prayerful time of meditation and a rhythmic peacefulness when tired, stressed, or in need of quiet, but it also centers us on the greatest mystery of our faith, namely that God chose to heal and save us through the humanity of his own Son, who was born of Mary, a real girl of a real town of Nazareth in the very land of the Bible itself. For centuries, we have prayed the fifteen traditional highlights of that salvation with deep devotion in union with Mary, but now Pope John Paul II has enriched that experience by expanding the mysteries we celebrate into five critical moments from the active ministry of Jesus as he taught and ministered to others. All of us should welcome these additions to our praying the Rosary because they touch us deeply where we live our Christian life each day as followers, disciples, and imitators of the Lord. This small book provides insightful verses of the Scriptures to accompany these new "mysteries of light" so that your own contemplation of redemption through God's Son will be joined even more closely with that of Mary, who in faith and in fear keenly followed every step of Jesus' saving ministry on earth.

Lawrence Boadt, C.S.P.

From Pope John Paul II's
Apostolic Letter

ROSARIUM VIRGINIS MARIAE

The Rosary of the Virgin Mary, which gradually took form in the second millennium under the guidance of the Spirit of God, is a prayer loved by countless Saints and encouraged by the Magisterium. Simple yet profound, it still remains, at the dawn of this third millennium, a prayer of great significance, destined to bring forth a harvest of holiness. It blends easily into the spiritual journey of the Christian life, which, after two thousand years, has lost none of the freshness of its beginnings and feels drawn by the Spirit of God to "set out into the deep" *(duc in altum!)* in order once more to proclaim, and even cry out, before the world that Jesus Christ is Lord and Saviour, "the way, and the truth and the life" (John 14:6), "the goal of human history and the point on which the desires of history and civilization turn" [*Gaudium et Spes*, 45].

The Rosary, though clearly Marian in character, is at heart a Christocentric prayer. In the sobriety of its elements, it has all the *depth of the Gospel message in its entirety,* of which it can be said to be a compendium. It is an echo of the prayer of Mary, her perennial *Magnificat* for the work of the redemptive Incarnation which began in her virginal womb. With the Rosary, the Christian people *[sit] at the school of Mary and [are]* led to contemplate the beauty on the face of Christ and to experience the depths of his love. Through the Rosary the faithful receive abundant grace, as though from the very hands of the Mother of the Redeemer.

Therefore, in continuity with my reflection in the Apostolic Letter *Novo Millennio Ineunte*, in which, after the experience of the Jubilee, I invited the people of God to "start afresh from Christ," I have felt drawn to offer a reflection on the Rosary, as a kind of Marian complement to that Letter and an exhortation to contemplate the face of Christ in union with, and at the school of, his Most Holy Mother. To recite the Rosary is nothing other than to *contemplate with Mary the face of Christ*. As a way of highlighting this invitation, prompted by the forthcoming 120th anniversary of the aforementioned Encyclical of Leo XIII, I desire that during the course of this year the Rosary should be especially emphasized and promoted in the various Christian communities. I therefore proclaim the year from October 2002 to October 2003 *the Year of the Rosary*.

The Rosary belongs among the finest and most praiseworthy traditions of Christian contemplation. Developed in the West, it is a typically meditative prayer, corresponding in some way to the "prayer of the heart" or "Jesus prayer" which took root in the soil of the Christian East.

A proposed addition to the traditional pattern

Of the many mysteries of Christ's life, only a few are indicated by the Rosary in the form that has become generally established with the seal of the Church's approval. The selection was determined by the origin of the prayer, which was based on the number 150, the number of the Psalms in the Psalter.

I believe, however, that to bring out fully the Christological depth of the Rosary it would be suitable to make an addition to the traditional pattern which, while left to the freedom of individuals and communities, could broaden it to include *the mysteries of Christ's public ministry between his Baptism and his Passion*. In the course of those mysteries we contemplate important aspects of the person of Christ as the definitive revelation of God. Declared the beloved Son of the Father at the Baptism in the Jordan, Christ is the one who announces the coming of the Kingdom, bears witness to it in his works and proclaims its demands. It is during the years of his public ministry that *the mystery of Christ is most evidently a mystery of light:* "While I am in the world, I am the light of the world" (John 9:5).

Consequently, for the Rosary to become more fully a "compendium of the Gospel," it is fitting to add, following reflection on the Incarnation and the hidden life of Christ *(the joyful mysteries)* and before focusing on the sufferings of his Passion *(the sorrowful mysteries)* and the triumph of his Resurrection *(the glorious mysteries)*, a meditation on certain particularly significant moments in his public ministry *(the mysteries of light)*. This addition of these new mysteries, without prejudice to any essential aspect of the prayer's traditional format, is meant to give it fresh life and to enkindle renewed interest in the Rosary's place within Christian spirituality as a true doorway to the depths of the Heart of Christ, ocean of joy and of light, of suffering and of glory.

From the Vatican, on the 16th day of October in the year 2002, the beginning of the twenty-fifth year of my Pontificate

JOHN PAUL II

Please see Appendix II for more from Pope John Paul II's Apostolic Letter

THE FIRST LUMINOUS MYSTERY:

The Baptism of Jesus in the Jordan

Christ descends into the waters, the innocent one who became "sin" for our own sake (cf. 2 Cor 5:21), the heavens open wide and the voice of the Father declares Him the beloved Son, while the Spirit descends on Him to invest Him with the mission which He is to carry out. —Pope John Paul II

Our Father

1. Then Jesus came from Galilee to John at the Jordan, to be baptized by him. John would have prevented him, saying, "I need to be baptized by you, and do you come to me?" But Jesus answered him, "Let it be so now; for it is proper for us in this way to fulfill all righteousness." Then he consented (Matt 3:13–15).

Hail Mary

2. Now when all the people were baptized, and when Jesus also had been baptized and was praying, the heaven was opened, and the Holy Spirit descended upon him in bodily form like a dove (Luke 3:21–22a).

Hail Mary

3. And a voice came from heaven, "You are my Son, the Beloved; with you I am well pleased" (Luke 3:22b).

Hail Mary

4. [John the Baptizer said] "But the one who sent me to baptize with water said to me, 'He on whom you see the Spirit descend and remain is the one who baptizes with the Holy Spirit.' And I myself have seen and have testified that this is the Son of God" (John 1:33b–34).

Hail Mary

5. John answered all of them by saying…."He will baptize you with the Holy Spirit and fire" (Luke 3:16).

Hail Mary

6. Jesus answered [Nicodemus], "Very truly, I tell you, no one can enter the kingdom of God without being born of water and Spirit. What is born of the flesh is flesh, and what is born of the Spirit is spirit" (John 3:5–6).

Hail Mary

7. And Jesus came and said to them, "All authority in heaven and on earth has been given to me. Go therefore and make disciples of all nations, baptizing them in the name of the Father and of the Son and of the Holy Spirit, and teaching them to obey everything that I have commanded you" (Matt 28:18–20a).

Hail Mary

8. And he said to them, "Go into all the world and proclaim the good news to the whole creation. The one who believes and is baptized will be saved" (Mark 16:15–16a).

Hail Mary

9. [Saint Paul wrote:] "For in Christ Jesus you are all children of God through faith. As many of you as were baptized into Christ have clothed

yourselves with Christ. Therefore....lead a life worthy of the calling to which you have been called" (Gal 3:26, 27; Eph 4:1b).

Hail Mary

10. When you were buried with him in baptism, you were also raised with him....For in the one Spirit we were all baptized into one body.... There is one body and one Spirit, just as you were called to the one hope of your calling, one Lord, one faith, one baptism, one God and Father of all, who is above all and through all and in all (Col 2:12a; 1 Cor 12:13a; Eph 4:4–6).

Hail Mary

For you are all children of light and children of the day; we are not of the night or of darkness (1 Thess 5:5).

Glory Be to the Father

THE SECOND LUMINOUS MYSTERY:

Jesus' Self-Manifestation at the Wedding at Cana

This Mystery of Light is the first of the signs, given at Cana (cf. John 2:1–12) when Christ changes water into wine and opens the hearts of the disciples to faith, thanks to the intercession of Mary, the first among believers.

—Pope John Paul II

Our Father

1. On the third day there was a wedding in Cana of Galilee, and the mother of Jesus was there. Jesus and his disciples had also been invited to the wedding (John 2:1–2).

Hail Mary

2. When the wine gave out, the mother of Jesus said to him, "They have no wine" (John 2:3).

Hail Mary

3. And Jesus said to her, "Woman, what concern is that to you and to me? My hour has not yet come" (John 2:4).

Hail Mary

4. His mother said to the servants, "Do whatever he tells you" (John 2:5).

Hail Mary

5. Now standing there were six stone water jars for the Jewish rites of purification, each holding twenty or thirty gallons. Jesus said to them, "Fill the jars with water." And they filled them up to the brim. He said to them, "Now draw some out, and take it to the chief steward." So they took it (John 2:6–8).

Hail Mary

6. When the steward tasted the water that had become wine, and did not know where it came from (though the servants who had drawn the

water knew), the steward called the bridegroom and said to him, "Everyone serves the good wine first, and then the inferior wine after the guests have become drunk. But you have kept the good wine until now" (John 2:9–10).

Hail Mary

7. Jesus did this, the first of his signs, in Cana of Galilee, and revealed his glory; and his disciples believed in him (John 2:11).

Hail Mary

8. Then he came again to Cana in Galilee where he had changed the water into wine. Now there was a royal official whose son lay ill in Capernaum. When he heard that Jesus had come from Judea to Galilee, he went and begged him to come down and heal his son, for he was at the point of death. Then Jesus said to him, "Unless you see signs and wonders you will not believe." Jesus' healed the official's son, and the official and his whole family came to believe (John 4:46–48; cf. John 4:53).

Hail Mary

9. [At the Last Supper when Jesus changed wine into His precious blood] He looked up to

heaven and said, "Father, the hour has come; glorify your Son so that the Son may glorify you" (John 17:1).

Hail Mary

10. [Jesus prayed:] "I glorified you on earth by finishing the work that you gave me to do. So now, Father, glorify me in your own presence with the glory that I had in your presence before the world existed. I have made your name known to those whom you gave me from the world. They were yours, and you gave them to me, and they have kept your word....For the words that you gave to me I have given to them, and they have received them and know in truth that I came from you; and they have believed that you sent me" (John 17:4–5, 6, 8).

Hail Mary

"Let us rejoice and exult and give him the glory, for the marriage of the Lamb has come, and his bride has made herself ready; to her it has been granted to be clothed with fine linen, bright and pure"—for the fine linen is the righteous deeds of the saints (Rev 19:7, 8)

Glory Be to the Father

THE THIRD LUMINOUS MYSTERY:

Jesus' Proclamation of the Kingdom of God with His Call to Conversion

In this Mystery of Light we contemplate the preaching by which Jesus proclaims the coming of the Kingdom of God, calls to conversion (cf. Mark 1:15) and forgives the sins of all who draw near to Him in humble trust (cf. Mark 2:2–13; Luke 7:47–48); the inauguration of that ministry of mercy which He continues to exercise until the end of the world, particularly through the Sacrament of Reconciliation which He entrusted to His Church (cf. John 20:22–23).

—Pope John Paul II

Our Father

1. Jesus came to Galilee, proclaiming the good news of God, and saying, "The time is fulfilled, and the kingdom of God has come near; repent, and believe in the good news" (Mark 1:14b–15).

Hail Mary

2. [On the Sabbath day, as was Jesus' custom] He stood up to read, and the scroll of the prophet Isaiah was given to him. He unrolled the scroll and found the place where it was written: "'The Spirit of the Lord is upon me, because he has anointed me to bring good news to the poor. He has sent me to proclaim release to the captives and recovery of sight to the blind, to let the oppressed go free....' Then he began to say to them, 'Today this scripture has been fulfilled in your hearing'" (Luke 4:16–18, 21).

Hail Mary

3. [Jesus said] "Do not think that I have come to abolish the law or the prophets; I have come not to abolish but to fulfill. Therefore, whoever breaks one of the least of these commandments, and teaches others to do the same, will be called

least in the kingdom of heaven; but whoever does them and teaches them will be called great in the kingdom of heaven" (Matt 5:17, 19).

Hail Mary

4. And [Jesus] said, "Truly I tell you, unless you change and become like children, you will never enter the kingdom of heaven. Whoever becomes humble like this child is the greatest in the kingdom of heaven" (Matt 18:3–4).

Hail Mary

5. "Pray then in this way: Our Father in heaven, hallowed be your name. Your kingdom come. Your will be done, on earth as it is in heaven" (Matt 6:9–10).

Hail Mary

6. "And I [Jesus] tell you, you are Peter, and on this rock I will build my church, and the gates of Hades will not prevail against it. I will give you the keys of the kingdom of heaven, and whatever you bind on earth will be bound in heaven, and whatever you loose on earth will be loosed in heaven" (Matt 16:18–19).

Hail Mary

7. "Blessed are the poor in spirit, for theirs is the kingdom of heaven. Blessed are those who mourn, for they will be comforted. Blessed are the meek, for they will inherit the earth. Blessed are those who hunger and thirst for righteousness, for they will be filled. Blessed are the merciful, for they will receive mercy. Blessed are the pure in heart, for they will see God. Blessed are the peacemakers, for they will be called children of God. Blessed are those who are persecuted for righteousness' sake, for theirs is the kingdom of heaven" (Matt 5:3–10).

Hail Mary

8. "Not everyone who says to me, 'Lord, Lord,' will enter the kingdom of heaven, but only the one who does the will of my Father in heaven" (Matt 7:21).

Hail Mary

9. "Come, you that are blessed by my Father, inherit the kingdom prepared for you from the foundation of the world....Truly I tell you, just as you did it to one of the least of these who are members of my family, you did it to me....Then the righteous will shine like the sun

in the kingdom of their Father" (Matt 25:34b, 40b; 13:43a).

Hail Mary

10. "Therefore I tell you, do not worry about your life, what you will eat, or about your body, what you will wear....your Father knows that you need them. Instead, strive for his kingdom, and these things will be given to you as well. Do not be afraid, little flock, for it is your Father's good pleasure to give you the kingdom" (Luke 12:22b, 30b–32).

Hail Mary

Giv[e] thanks to the Father, who has enabled you to share in the inheritance of the saints in the light. He has rescued us from the power of darkness and transferred us into the kingdom of his beloved Son, in whom we have redemption, the forgiveness of sins (Col 1:12–14).

Glory Be to the Father

The Transfiguration of Jesus

The Mystery of Light par excellence is the Transfiguration, traditionally believed to have taken place on Mount Tabor. The glory of the Godhead shines forth from the face of Christ as the Father commands the astonished apostles to "Listen to Him" (cf. Luke 9:35) and prepare to experience with Him the agony of the passion, so as to come with Him to the joy of the Resurrection and the life transfigured by the Holy Spirit.

—Pope John Paul II

Our Father

1. Jesus took with him Peter and James and his brother John and led them up a high mountain, by themselves. And he was transfigured before

them, and his face shone like the sun, and his clothes became dazzling white (Matt 17:1–2).

Hail Mary

2. Suddenly they saw two men, Moses and Elijah, talking to him. They appeared in glory and were speaking of his departure, which he was about to accomplish at Jerusalem (Luke 9:30–31).

Hail Mary

3. Then Peter said to Jesus, "Rabbi, it is good for us to be here!" Then a cloud overshadowed them, and from the cloud there came a voice, "This is my Son, the Beloved; listen to him!" (Mark 9:5a, 7).

Hail Mary

4. As they were coming down the mountain, he ordered them to tell no one about what they had seen, until after the Son of Man had risen from the dead (Mark 9:9).

Hail Mary

5. [Later Saint Peter wrote:] "We had been eyewitnesses of his majesty....We ourselves

heard this voice come from heaven, while we were with him on the holy mountain. So we have the prophetic message more fully confirmed" (2 Peter 1:16b, 18, 19a).

Hail Mary

6. You will do well to be attentive to this as to a lamp shining in a dark place, until the day dawns and the morning star rises in your hearts (2 Peter 1:19b).

Hail Mary

7. For salvation is nearer to us now than when we became believers; the night is far gone, the day is near. Let us then lay aside the works of darkness and put on the armor of light; let us live honorably as in the day, and....put on the Lord Jesus Christ (Rom 13:11b, 12, 13a, 14a).

Hail Mary

8. For once you were darkness, but now in the Lord you are light. Live as children of light—for the fruit of the light is found in all that is good and right and true. Try to find out what is pleasing to the Lord (Eph 5:8–10).

Hail Mary

9. He is the reflection of God's glory and the exact imprint of God's very being....He will transform the body of our humiliation that it may be conformed to the body of his glory (Heb 1:3; Phil 3:21a).

Hail Mary

10. And all of us, with unveiled faces, seeing the glory of the Lord as though reflected in a mirror, are being transformed into the same image from one degree of glory to another; for this comes from the Lord, the Spirit....For it is the God who said, "Let light shine out of darkness," who has shone in our hearts to give the light of the knowledge of the glory of God in the face of Jesus Christ (2 Cor 3:18; 4:6).

Hail Mary

Let your light shine before others, so that they may see your good works and give glory to your Father in heaven (Matt 5:16).

Glory Be to the Father

THE FIFTH LUMINOUS MYSTERY:

Jesus Institutes the Eucharist as the Sacramental Expression of the Paschal Mystery

The final Mystery of Light is the institution of the Eucharist, in which Christ offers his body and blood as food under the signs of bread and wine, and testifies "to the end" His love for humanity (John 13:1), for whose salvation He will offer Himself in sacrifice. —*Pope John Paul II*

Our Father

1. Now before the festival of the Passover, Jesus knew that his hour had come to depart from this world and go to the Father. Having loved his

24

own who were in the world, he loved them to the end (John 13:1).

Hail Mary

2. When the hour came, he took his place at the table, and the apostles with him. He said to them, "I have eagerly desired to eat this Passover with you before I suffer; for I tell you, I will not eat it until it is fulfilled in the kingdom of God" (Luke 22:14–16).

Hail Mary

3. While they were eating, Jesus took a loaf of bread, and after blessing it he broke it, gave it to the disciples, and said, "Take, eat; this is my body" (Matt 26:26).

Hail Mary

4. Then he took a cup, and after giving thanks he gave it to them, saying, "Drink from it, all of you; for this is my blood of the covenant, which is poured out for many for the forgiveness of sins....Do this in remembrance of me" (Matt 26:27–28. Luke 22:19b).

Hail Mary

5. For as often as you eat this bread and drink the cup, you proclaim the Lord's death until he comes (1 Cor 11:26).

Hail Mary

6. "I am the living bread that came down from heaven. Whoever eats of this bread will live forever; and the bread that I will give for the life of the world is my flesh....Those who eat my flesh and drink my blood have eternal life, and I will raise them up on the last day" (John 6:51, 54).

Hail Mary

7. "For my flesh is true food and my blood is true drink. Those who eat my flesh and drink my blood abide in me, and I in them. Just as the living Father sent me, and I live because of the Father, so whoever eats me will live because of me" (John 6:55–57).

Hail Mary

8. Now on that same day two of them were going to a village called Emmaus, about seven miles from Jerusalem, and talking with each other about all these things that had happened. While

they were talking and discussing, Jesus himself came near and went with them, but their eyes were kept from recognizing him....Then beginning with Moses and all the prophets, Jesus interpreted to them the things about himself in all the scriptures....When he was at the table with them, he took bread, blessed and broke it, and gave it to them. Then their eyes were opened, and they recognized him....They said to each other, "Were not our hearts burning within us while he was talking to us on the road, while he was opening the scriptures to us?" (Luke 24:13–16, 27, 30–31a, 32).

Hail Mary

9. The cup of blessing that we bless, is it not a sharing in the blood of Christ? The bread that we break, is it not a sharing in the body of Christ? (1 Cor 10:16).

Hail Mary

10. Like living stones, let yourselves be built into a spiritual house, to be a holy priesthood, to offer spiritual sacrifices acceptable to God through Jesus Christ....You are a chosen race, a royal priesthood, a holy nation, God's own people, in order that you may proclaim the

mighty acts of him who called you out of darkness into his marvelous light (1 Peter 2:5, 9).

Hail Mary

For from the rising of the sun to its setting my name is great among the nations, and in every place incense is offered to my name, and a pure offering; for my name is great among the nations, says the LORD of hosts (Mal 1:11).

Glory Be to the Father

Appendix I

How to Pray the Rosary

1. Make the Sign of the Cross and say the Apostles' Creed while holding the crucifix.
2. On the first large bead after the crucifix, say the Our Father.
3. On each of the next three small beads, say one Hail Mary (traditionally one for each of the "Theological Virtues": Faith, Hope, and Love).
4. On the space between the third small bead and the next large bead, say the Glory Be to the Father.
5. While holding the next large bead, announce the First Mystery, then say the Our Father.
6. Say ten Hail Marys, one on each of the small beads.
7. Say the Glory Be to the Father on the space between the last small bead and the next large bead.
8. Announce the Second Mystery, then, say the Our Father while holding the next large bead.

9. Repeat steps 6 and 7 for the Second, Third, Fourth, and Fifth Mysteries.

After the Fifth Mystery, any of the following prayers may be recited to finish the Rosary.

The Memorare

Remember, Most loving Virgin Mary, never was it heard that anyone who turned to you for help was left unaided. Inspired by this confidence, though burdened by my sins, I run to your protection, for you are my mother. O Mother of the Word of God, do not despise my words of pleading, but be merciful and hear my prayer. Amen.

The Salve Regina

mother of mercy Hail

Hail, holy Queen, our life, our sweetness and our hope! To thee do we cry, poor, banished children of Eve. To thee do we send up our sighs, mourning and weeping in this valley of tears. Turn, then, *oh* most gracious advocate, thine eyes of mercy toward us. And after this our exile, show unto us the blessed fruit of thy womb, Jesus. O clement, O loving, O sweet Virgin Mary.

Pray for us, *oh* Holy Mother of God: That we may be made worthy of the promises of Christ. Amen.

Closing Prayer

Let us pray:

O God, whose only-begotten Son by His life, death, and resurrection has purchased for us the rewards of eternal life, grant, we beseech thee, that by meditating on the mysteries of the most holy Rosary of the Blessed Virgin Mary, we may both imitate what they contain and obtain what they promise, through the same Christ Our Lord. Amen.

Optional Prayers

In addition to the Glory Be to the Father that follows the end of each decade of the Rosary, the following prayer may be recited:

O my Jesus forgive us our sins

O my Jesus, ~~have mercy on us all~~. Save us from the fires of hell. Lead all souls to Heaven, especially those who have most need of Thy mercy. Amen.

At the end of the Rosary, the following prayer may be said:

Loving Mother of the Redeemer, Gate of Heaven, Star of the Sea:
Assist your people who have fallen, yet strive to rise again. To the wonderment of nature you

31

bore your Creator, Yet you remained a virgin after as before.
You who received Gabriel's joyful greeting,
Have pity on us poor sinners. Amen.

Also, an Our Father, three Hail Marys and a Glory Be to the Father may be said for the intentions of the pope right after one finishes praying the Rosary.

ROSARIUM VIRGINIS MARIAE

The Popes and the Rosary

Numerous predecessors of mine attributed great importance to this prayer. Worthy of special note in this regard is Pope Leo XIII who on 1 September 1883 promulgated the Encyclical *Supremi Apostolatus Officio*, a document of great worth, the first of his many statements about this prayer, in which he proposed the Rosary as an effective spiritual weapon against the evils afflicting society. Among the more recent Popes who, from the time of the Second Vatican Council, have distinguished themselves in promoting the Rosary I would mention Blessed John XXIII and above all Pope Paul VI, who in his Apostolic Exhortation *Marialis Cultus* emphasized, in the spirit of the Second Vatican Council, the Rosary's evangelical character and its Christocentric inspiration. I myself have often encouraged the frequent recitation of the Rosary. From my youthful years this prayer has held an important place in my spiritual life. I was powerfully reminded of this during my recent visit to Poland, and in particular at the Shrine of Kalwaria. The Rosary has accompanied me in moments of joy and in moments of difficulty. To it I have entrusted any number of concerns; in it I have always found comfort. Twenty-four years ago, on 29 October 1978, scarcely two weeks after my election to the See of Peter, I frankly admitted: "The Rosary is my favourite prayer. A marvellous prayer! Marvellous in its simplicity and its depth. [...]. It can be said that the Rosary is, in some sense, a prayer-commentary on the final chapter of the Vatican II Constitution *Lumen Gentium*, a chapter which discusses the wondrous presence of the Mother of God in the mystery of Christ and the Church. Against the background of the words *Ave Maria* the principal events of the life of Jesus Christ pass before the eyes of the soul. They take shape in the complete series of the joyful, sorrowful and glorious mysteries, and they put us in living communion with Jesus through—we might say—the heart of his Mother. At the same time our heart can embrace in the decades of the Rosary all the events that make up the lives of individuals, families, nations, the Church, and all mankind.

Our personal concerns and those of our neigh-
bour, especially those who are closest to us, who
are dearest to us. Thus the simple prayer of the
Rosary marks the rhythm of human life."

With these words, dear brothers and sis-
ters, I set *the first year of my Pontificate* within
the daily rhythm of the Rosary. Today, *as I begin
the twenty-fifth year of my service as the
Successor of Peter*, I wish to do the same. How
many graces have I received in these years from
the Blessed Virgin through the Rosary:
Magnificat anima mea Dominum! I wish to lift
up my thanks to the Lord in the words of his
Most Holy Mother, under whose protection I
have placed my Petrine ministry: *Totus Tuus!*

The Rosary beads

The traditional aid used for the recitation of the
Rosary is the set of beads. At the most superficial
level, the beads often become a simple counting
mechanism to mark the succession of Hail
Marys. Yet they can also take on a symbolism
which can give added depth to contemplation.

Here the first thing to note is the way *the
beads converge upon the Crucifix*, which both
opens and closes the unfolding sequence of
prayer. The life and prayer of believers is centered
upon Christ. Everything begins from him, every-

thing leads towards him, everything, through him, in the Holy Spirit, attains to the Father.

As a counting mechanism, marking the progress of the prayer, the beads evoke the unending path of contemplation and of Christian perfection. Blessed Bartolo Longo saw them also as a "chain" which links us to God. A chain, yes, but a sweet chain; for sweet indeed is the bond to God who is also our Father. A "filial" chain which puts us in tune with Mary, the "handmaid of the Lord" (Luke 1:38) and, most of all, with Christ himself, who, though he was in the form of God, made himself a "servant" out of love for us (Phil 2:7).

The opening and closing

At present, in different parts of the Church, there are many ways to introduce the Rosary. In some places, it is customary to begin with the opening words of Psalm 70: "O God, come to my aid; O Lord, make haste to help me," as if to nourish in those who are praying a humble awareness of their own insufficiency. In other places, the Rosary begins with the recitation of the Creed, as if to make the profession of faith the basis of the contemplative journey about to be undertaken. These and similar customs, to the extent that they prepare the mind for contemplation, are all equally legitimate. The Rosary is then ended

36

with a prayer for the intentions of the Pope, as if to expand the vision of the one praying to embrace all the needs of the Church. It is precisely in order to encourage this ecclesial dimension of the Rosary that the Church has seen fit to grant indulgences to those who recite it with the required dispositions.

Distribution over time

The Rosary can be recited in full every day, and there are those who most laudably do so. In this way it fills with prayer the days of many a contemplative, or keeps company with the sick and the elderly who have abundant time at their disposal. Yet it is clear—and this applies all the more if the new series of *mysteria lucis* is included—that many people will not be able to recite more than a part of the Rosary, according to a certain weekly pattern. This weekly distribution has the effect of giving the different days of the week a certain spiritual "colour," by analogy with the way in which the Liturgy colours the different seasons of the liturgical year.

According to current practice, Monday and Thursday are dedicated to the "joyful mysteries," Tuesday and Friday to the "sorrowful mysteries," and Wednesday, Saturday and Sunday to the "glorious mysteries." Where might the "mysteries of light" be inserted? If we consider that the "glorious mysteries" are said on both Saturday and Sunday, and that Saturday has always had a special Marian flavour, the second weekly meditation on the "joyful mysteries," mysteries in which Mary's presence is especially pronounced, could be moved to Saturday. Thursday would then be free for meditating on the "mysteries of light."

This indication is not intended to limit a rightful freedom in personal and community prayer, where account needs to be taken of spiritual and pastoral needs and of the occurrence of particular liturgical celebrations which might call for suitable adaptations. What is really important is that the Rosary should always be seen and experienced as a path of contemplation. In the Rosary, in a way similar to what takes place in the Liturgy, the Christian week, centered on Sunday, the day of Resurrection, becomes a journey through the mysteries of the life of Christ, and he is revealed in the lives of his disciples as the Lord of time and of history.

CONCLUSION

"Blessed Rosary of Mary, sweet chain linking us to God"

What has been said so far makes abundantly clear the richness of this traditional prayer, which has the simplicity of a popular devotion but also the theological depth of a prayer suited to those who feel the need for deeper contemplation.

The Church has always attributed particular efficacy to this prayer, entrusting to the Rosary, to its choral recitation and to its constant practice, the most difficult problems. At times when Christianity itself seemed under threat, its deliverance was attributed to the power of this prayer, and Our Lady of the Rosary was acclaimed as the one whose intercession brought salvation.

Today I willingly entrust to the power of this prayer—as I mentioned at the beginning— the cause of peace in the world and the cause of the family.

The family: parents...

As a prayer for peace, the Rosary is also, and always has been, *a prayer of and for the family*. At one time this prayer was particularly dear to Christian families, and it certainly brought them closer together. It is important not to lose this precious inheritance. We need to return to the practice of family prayer and prayer for families, continuing to use the Rosary.

In my Apostolic Letter *Novo Millennio Ineunte* I encouraged the celebration of the

Liturgy of the Hours by the lay faithful in the ordinary life of parish communities and Christian groups; I now wish to do the same for the Rosary. These two paths of Christian contemplation are not mutually exclusive; they complement one another. I would therefore ask those who devote themselves to the pastoral care of families to recommend heartily the recitation of the Rosary.

The family that prays together stays together. The Holy Rosary, by age-old tradition, has shown itself particularly effective as a prayer which brings the family together. Individual family members, in turning their eyes towards Jesus, also regain the ability to look one another in the eye, to communicate, to show solidarity, to forgive one another and to see their covenant of love renewed in the Spirit of God.

Many of the problems facing contemporary families, especially in economically developed societies, result from their increasing difficulty in communicating. Families seldom manage to come together, and the rare occasions when they do are often taken up with watching television. To return to the recitation of the family Rosary means filling daily life with very different images, images of the mystery of salvation: the image of the Redeemer, the image of his most Blessed Mother. The family that recites the Rosary together reproduces something of the atmosphere of the household of Nazareth: its members place Jesus at the centre, they share his joys and sorrows, they place their needs and their plans in his hands, they draw from him the hope and the strength to go on.

...and children

It is also beautiful and fruitful to entrust to this prayer *the growth and development of children*. Does the Rosary not follow the life of Christ, from his conception to his death, and then to his Resurrection and his glory? Parents are finding it ever more difficult to follow the lives of their children as they grow to maturity. In a society of advanced technology, of mass communications and globalization, everything has become hurried, and the cultural distance between generations is growing ever greater. The most diverse messages and the most unpredictable experiences rapidly make their way into the lives of children and adolescents, and parents can become quite anxious about the dangers their children face. At times parents suffer acute disappointment at the failure of their children to resist the seductions of the drug culture, the lure of an unbridled hedonism, the temptation to violence, and the manifold expressions of mean-inglessness and despair.

To pray the Rosary *for children*, and even more, *with children*, training them from their earliest years to experience this daily "pause for prayer" with the family, is admittedly not the solution to every problem, but it is a spiritual aid which should not be underestimated. It could be objected that the Rosary seems hardly suited to the taste of children and young people of today. But perhaps the objection is directed to an impoverished method of praying it. Further-more, without prejudice to the Rosary's basic structure, there is nothing to stop children and young people from praying it—either within the family or in groups—with appropriate symbolic and practical aids to understanding and appre-ciation. Why not try it? With God's help, a pas-toral approach to youth which is positive, impassioned and creative—as shown by the World Youth Days!—is capable of achieving quite remarkable results. If the Rosary is well presented, I am sure that young people will once more surprise adults by the way they make this prayer their own and recite it with the enthusi-asm typical of their age group.

May this appeal of mine not go unheard! At the start of the twenty-fifth year of my Pontificate,

I entrust this Apostolic Letter to the loving hands of the Virgin Mary, *prostrating myself in spirit before her image in the splendid Shrine built for her by Blessed Bartolo Longo,* the apostle of the Rosary. I willingly make my own the touching words with which he concluded his well-known *Supplication to the Queen of the Holy Rosary:* "O Blessed Rosary of Mary, sweet chain which unites us to God, bond of love which unites us to the angels, tower of salvation against the assaults of Hell, safe port in our universal shipwreck, we will never abandon you. You will be our comfort in the hour of death: yours our final kiss as life ebbs away. And the last word from our lips will be your sweet name, O Queen of the Rosary of Pompei, O dearest Mother, O Refuge of Sinners, O Sovereign Consoler of the Afflicted. May you be everywhere blessed, today and always, on earth and in heaven."

From the Vatican, on the 16th day of October in the year 2002, the beginning of the twenty-fifth year of my Pontificate.

JOHN PAUL II